A Year of Borrowed Men

BY MICHELLE BARKER

ILLUSTRATED BY RENNÉ BENOIT

PAJAMAPRESS

First published in the United States in 2016
First published in Canada in 2015

Text copyright © 2015 Michelle Barker
Illustrations copyright © 2015 Renné Benoit
This edition copyright © 2015 Pajama Press Inc.
This is a first edition.

10 9 8 7 6 5 4 3 2 1

www.pajamapress.ca   info@pajamapress.ca

Canada Council   Conseil des arts   ONTARIO ARTS COUNCIL
for the Arts   du Canada   CONSEIL DES ARTS DE L'ONTARIO   Canada
                                            an Ontario government agency
                                            un organisme du gouvernement de l'Ontario

The publisher gratefully acknowledges the support of the Canada Council for the Arts and the
Ontario Arts Council for its publishing program. We acknowledge the financial support of the
Government of Canada through the Canada Book Fund (CBF) for our publishing activities.

Library and Archives Canada Cataloguing in Publication

Barker, Michelle, 1964 - .
   A year of borrowed men / by Michelle Barker ; illustrated by Renné Benoit.
[40] pages : color illustrations, photographs ; cm.
Summary: "When World War II 'borrows' most of the men in Germany, six-year-old Gerda's family is
allowed to borrow three French prisoners of war to help run their farm. They are supposed to treat
the men as enemies, but the family finds clever ways to show kindness and friendship. Based on a
true story" – Provided by publisher.
ISBN-13: 978-1-92748-583-5
1. World War, 1939-1945 – Prisoners and prisons, German – Juvenile fiction. 2. World War, 1939-
1945 – Children – Juvenile fiction. I. Benoit, Renné, 1977 - . II. Title.
[E] dc23   PZ7.1.B375Yr 2015

Publisher Cataloging-in-Publication Data (U.S.)

Barker, Michelle, 1964 - .
   A year of borrowed men / by Michelle Barker ; illustrated by Renné Benoit.
[40] pages : color illustrations, photographs ; cm.
Summary: "When World War II 'borrows' most of the men in Germany, six-year-old Gerda's family is
allowed to borrow three French prisoners of war to help run their farm. They are supposed to treat
the men as enemies, but the family finds clever ways to show kindness and friendship. Based on a
true story" – Provided by publisher.
ISBN-13: 978-1-92748-583-5
1. World War, 1939-1945 – Prisoners and prisons, German – Juvenile fiction. 2. World War, 1939-
1945 – Children – Juvenile fiction. I. Benoit, Renné, 1977 - . II. Title.
[E] dc23   PZ7.1.B375Yr 2015

Cover and book design—Rebecca Bender
Manufactured by Qualibre Inc./Print Plus
Printed in China

Pajama Press Inc.
181 Carlaw Ave. Suite 207 Toronto, Ontario Canada, M4M 2S1

Distributed in Canada by UTP Distribution
5201 Dufferin Street Toronto, Ontario Canada, M3H 5T8

Distributed in the U.S. by Ingram Publisher Services
1 Ingram Blvd. La Vergne, TN 37086, USA

The illustrations are rendered in watercolour and coloured pencil, with a little pastel, on paper.

*The house and farm in
Beelkow, Germany, where
Gerda lived during the war*

I was seven when the French prisoners of war arrived at our house.

It was 1944. Mummy told us the government had sent them because all our men were gone to war, and someone needed to keep the farms running. She said we were just borrowing the French men. When the war was over, we would give them back.

I was glad they were here, because the war had already borrowed Papi. We were a big family: five children plus Mummy. But Franz was the only boy and he was still just a teenager. We needed the help. We had cows, pigs, 150 chickens, and six horses to pull carriages and help with work in the field. We were lucky compared to others in our German village. We had milk and butter, meat, eggs, and produce to sell to people in the nearby city. But it was a lot to take care of.

We called the borrowed men our French family: gentle Gabriel, prickly Fermaine, and cheerful Albert, who loved games. I wanted them to live with us in our house, but Mummy said it was *verboten* (forbidden).

"We're supposed to treat them like prisoners, Gerda," she explained.

"But it's not fair, making them sleep in the pig kitchen," I said.

The pig kitchen was where we cooked potatoes for the pigs. It was right next to where the animals slept, and smelled like manure. It wasn't meant for people. When the borrowed men ate, they sat on wobbly chairs in the pig kitchen and used a big box as their table.

One day when it was very cold, I felt sorry for the borrowed men and invited them to eat with us. Our kitchen had a wood and coal burning stove, and a table big enough for friends. The borrowed men knew some German words but we did not speak French. We had to use our hands to show them what we meant. Sometimes I drew pictures for them.

One of the neighbors must have seen us at the table together.

The next day we heard a knock at the door.

You always knew it was the village policeman by the way he knocked: a hard, important *RAP*. Everyone knew Herr Mohlen from the days when he used to be kind. But since the war began, he had changed, and we knew enough to be afraid of him. I stood close to my sister Christa, and my knees felt funny when he said, "*Frau Schlottke, kommen Sie mit.*" (Mrs. Schlottke, come with me.)

"Why are they borrowing Mummy?" I whispered.

Christa shushed me while Mummy put on her woolen coat.

I was afraid we might not see her again, but she came
back later that day. We crowded around her, all of us
asking, "What happened?"

"Once more," she said, "and they'll put me in prison."

Our borrowed men stayed in the pig kitchen after that.

Every day the borrowed men went out to the fields to help run the horse plow or milk the cows. It was my job to bring them lunch. Mummy would pack up one of our horses, and I would lead her out toward the fields. The horse always knew where the men were. I just followed.

They were happy to see me. Whenever they milked
the cows, they filled a tin cup of warm milk for me.
Sometimes they squirted the milk right into my mouth.

Mummy baked all our bread, in huge ovens, fifty loaves at a time. She smoked the ham, which came from our pigs. When she made sandwiches for the men, she used lots of butter. She was determined to feed them well.

Soon it was Christmas. The borrowed men were allowed a small Christmas tree, but we weren't supposed to give them decorations and they could not have lit candles like we had on our tree.

The borrowed men looked forward to the catalogs we received in the mail, which displayed all the new coats and boots you could buy if you had money. They liked to look at the pictures. It gave me an idea. I cut out some of the pictures and asked Mummy for a needle and thread.

"A Christmas tree should be pretty," I said.

Mummy also gave me tinsel to take to the men, and a box filled with *Lebkuchen* she had baked. Putting one finger to her lips, she reminded me to keep quiet. I helped Fermaine, Albert, and Gabriel decorate their catalog Christmas tree.

On Christmas Eve we ate a cold dinner of Tunisian salad. We sang songs around the tree and then opened our presents. Mummy had bought me a doll, my first real one ever. Before, I had only made dolls out of the clay that I dug from outside.

Oh, how I loved my new doll. She had blue eyes that opened and shut, and such real-looking hands and feet.

I took my doll to the pig kitchen to show the borrowed men. They were sitting on their wobbly chairs telling stories. Their language sounded like velvet.

"*Eine Puppe*," I said to them.

"*Une poupée*," they said.

It was almost the same.

My doll was so cold. While the men talked and laughed I decided to warm her up on the stove. I left her for just a few minutes.

Suddenly Albert yelled, "*Gerda, ta poupée!*" (Gerda, your doll!)

By the time I picked her up, her hands and feet had melted to stubs. I cried and cried, but Gabriel put bandages on her to make her better.

On Christmas day the house smelled of roasted goose, which Mummy baked with prunes to make it sweet. She made potatoes and gravy, and a compote of pumpkin with cloves, nutmeg, and vinegar. The borrowed men were not allowed to have Christmas dinner with us, but my brother and I went to the pig kitchen and traded them compote for some nougat they'd received in a parcel.

"*Amis*," Albert said.   He put his arms around Fermaine and Gabriel, and they held out their hands to us.

"Ah," said my brother. "*Freunde*."

We took their hands. We were friends, *Freunde*. How close it was to *Feinde* (enemies).

I handed my doll to Albert, and he rocked her to sleep.

The war was over by springtime. The borrowed men yelled, "*Libération*!" (Freedom) It was time to give them back. Russian soldiers ran through our village opening all the barns. Even the animals were free. Our herd of cows ran away, which meant no more milk or butter for us. And now our pig kitchen was so quiet.

One day, we ran into Albert and Gabriel on the road.
They weren't prisoners anymore. Albert put his hands
together over his head like a roof. They were going home.

I felt sad, but Albert smiled and held his arms out to me.

"*Amis*," he said.

I couldn't keep the borrowed men here, but we were friends—and I could keep that forever. I hugged him and Gabriel.

"*Freunde*," I answered.

A Year of Borrowed Men is based on a true story. My mother grew up in Germany during the Second World War, and in 1944 her family was obliged by the Nazi government to take French prisoners of war into their home so that they could continue to operate their farm. The rules were strict. German families were instructed to treat these men as prisoners, not as members of the family. The consequences of disobeying the rules were grave: you could be put in prison. Neighbors were told to keep their eyes and ears open for anyone who didn't follow the rules. But people like my mother and her family found ways to be kind to these men, despite the danger they faced if they were caught.

The war had borrowed my mother's father, and later, her brother Franz. My mother and her family waited for the war to give the men back. But it never happened. She lost both her brother and her father.

At the age of seventeen, my mother escaped from East Germany and immigrated to Canada four years later to join her sister. They settled in British Columbia. Years later, my mother was able to return to Germany to see her mother before she died.

My mother never forgot the time her family spent with the French prisoners of war. Though she never saw them again, she remembered their kindness and often imagined them home in France with their families, cutting out catalog pictures to hang on their Christmas trees.

*Top: Gerda, aged 10, 1946. **Middle:** The five Schlottke siblings (from front to back), Gerda, Brunhilde, Franz, Christa, and Edith, 1942. **Bottom:** Mummy, Papi, and Baby Edith, 1921.*

All photos courtesy of the Schlottke family